Itzik Oron

Yoga Story

All Rights Reserved

Itzik Oron, 2020

All rights, in any language, belong to the author Itzik Oron

Email: itzakoron@gmail.com

Website: www.itzakoron.022.co.il

Editor: Hagar Yanai

Translated from Hebrew: Grace Michaeli

The plots, characters, and names are all figments of the author's imagination.
Any relation between the plots and real-life occurrences, as well as between the characters and
any living or deceased person, is entirely coincidental.

Do not copy, duplicate, photograph, record, translate, store in a database,
broadcast, or receive, in any way – electronic, optic,
mechanical or otherwise – any part of this book.
Any commercial use of anything in this book, of any kind, is strictly
prohibited, unless explicitly authorized by the author.

Design and pagination: Lev Ari Studio

Illustrations: Michal Zinger

Shachar Laudon

Printed in Israel, August 2020

ORON

Dear parents and children:

I wrote the book *Yoga Story 1* with great love for the thousands of children I have taught in recent years, and to share the experience I gained teaching thousands of yoga classes to these wonderful children.

The great pleasure I experienced when I saw the spark in the eyes of my young students, as they practiced with me using the fascinating stories I wrote for them, was the greatest salary I could ever ask for – and it motivated me to put those stories into a book.

I would like to thank all the dear people who took part in the fulfillment of my dream to write this book, and especially I thank my dear six-year-old student Sivan Zahovitsky, who stars in my book with professionalism and great grace.

I believe and wish you will have a wondrous experience from the moment you enter the yoga world.

With big love,
Itzik Oron– writer and yoga teacher

Table of Contents

Recommendations on how to use the book . . 5

The Elephant Who Wasn't Afraid of the Lion . . 6

Shawana the Brave Dog 10

The Camel and the Giant Bamboo Tree . . . 14

The Brave Bees 18

The Eagle and the Pigeon. 22

The Noble Swan 26

The Warrior Who Guarded the Forest . . . 30

The Animal Farm 34

Half-Moon 38

The Golden-Winged Crane 42

Terms dictionary 46

Recommendations on how to use the book:

- In every story, names of animals or objects appear in red type, along with a matching picture that gives instructions for a yoga pose. When you reach a word in **red**, you should stop the story and perform the corresponding yoga pose. For instance, when the word **"Rabbit"** appears in red, locate the image labeled **"Rabbit"** and perform the pose shown, with either the child or grown-up counting the breaths. (A deep inhale and exhale equals one breath.)

- You should start from the lowest difficulty and gradually go up.

- It is recommended that you read the stories in order and not skip any of them. Practice the poses in the order in which they appear in each story.

- We recommend going through the first six stories at least twice, before moving on to the other six.

- However, it's best not to practice more than one story a day, and to take at least one day off between stories, without any practice. This will keep children from tiring of Yoga and also allow their muscles to rest.

- You should be aware of balance, practice both sides of the body equally, and stay in each pose for three to six complete breaths—following the instructions below each picture while considering the child's ability as well.

- Inhaling and exhaling are always done through the nose.

- The child pictured in the book is Sivan. She spent about six months practicing with me as part of a class I gave at her preschool.

Game recommendation:

At the end of practice, invite one of the children whose skills stood out to come to the Yoga instructor's or parent's mat. Let that child choose one or two poses from the story and lead the other students. The other students need to perform the pose according to the leader's instructions. The child leading can then choose the student they think performed the poses best and make them the next instructor. The first child who instructed goes back to their own mat and follows the new instructor, who, when finished, chooses another child to come up and lead, and so on.

Elephant trunk up
Inhale, hands up

Elephant trunk down
Exhale, lean down

Rabbit
Inhale, head down, hold for 5 breaths

Lion
Sit on heels, back straight, extend tongue while inhaling and roar

The Elephant Who Wasn't Afraid of the Lion

In a wide forest lived a big and smart **Elephant**, who was friends with all the good animals.

One morning, the elephant arrived at the river, as he usually did, to bathe and drink water. He dipped his trunk in the river in **Elephant's Trunk Pose**, filled it with water, lifted it up, and drank, gulp-gulp-gulp.

The **Elephant** dipped his trunk again and filled it with water, but this time he sprayed it, on his back and on his legs, until he was very clean.

The third time, as the **Elephant** looked down to fill up his trunk again, he saw his friend the **Rabbit** between his legs.

"Rabbit-buddy, my friend, why are you between my legs?" the elephant asked his rabbit friend.

"I am hiding from the bad lion who wants to eat me. Please save me," the rabbit fearfully said. As he begged for help, the cruel **Lion** appeared, revealed his long sharp claws, bore his huge teeth, and roared "Grrrr," to scare the giant elephant and the little rabbit.

"Don't worry rabbit-buddy, stay between my legs," the elephant said. The **Elephant** kept standing, and instead of fleeing, he dipped his trunk in the river and filled it with water. Without fearing the grumpy lion, he lifted his trunk up, sprayed the water on the lion, and got him all soaked.

The lion became even angrier and decided to roar even louder– maybe this time the elephant would get scared and run away, and he could finally eat the rabbit.

The **Lion** got on his hind legs, breathed in to fill his lungs, and then roared as hard as he could: "Grrrrrrrr," with a deafening sound, sticking his tongue out as he roared.

Rabbit
Inhale, head down, hold for 5 breaths

Elephant trunk up
Inhale, hands up

Elephant trunk down
Exhale, lean down

The **Rabbit** was so scared he almost fainted, but he calmed down when he saw his good friend the giant **Elephant** lowering his long trunk into the river, filling it with water again – a lot of water this time. Then he lifted it and sprayed all the water on the cruel lion: "Pshshshshshsh." The lion, who almost drowned in the giant puddle made by the elephant, got really scared, jumped up, and ran away.

The **Rabbit** sighed in relief. He was so happy he was saved. He bowed in thanks to his friend the giant elephant, and said: "Thank you very much, my friend the elephant, for saving me."

The elephant replied: "You are welcome, my friend. Run home and hide in your burrow because the lion might come back, and I will not be here to protect you." The rabbit took his friend's advice and started running fast towards the top of the **Mountain** to warn his friend the turtle, and tell him about how he was saved from the lion.

The rabbit reached the giant **Tree**, where his friend the **Turtle** liked to rest. All excited, he told the turtle what had happened and how he was saved from the evil lion, and before he went to his burrow, he warned the turtle, "My friend the turtle, you must be careful and hide from the lion, for he might come here, too."

The **Turtle** heard the story and got so scared that he couldn't lift his head from between his legs.

Mountain
Body held straight and stretched, look towards palms, hold for 8 breaths

Tree
Sole of foot on thigh, hands up, hold for 5 breaths for each foot

Turtle
Hold position while inhaling for 5 breaths

Luckily for the turtle, the **Butterfly** was sitting on the top of the giant **Tree**, with her friend the pigeon. She heard the conversation between the two friends and decided to help the worried turtle calm down. She flew down and landed on his nose, waved her wings, and whispered in his ear: "Don't be afraid, turtle, the lion could never eat you – your shell is too hard."

The turtle relaxed and started to smile. Then he started to laugh in relief. He thanked his friend the **Butterfly**, and once she saw the turtle was relaxed, she flew back up to the top of the **Tree**, to her friend the **Pigeon**. The pigeon listened to what had happened and complimented his friend, "Well done, butterfly, for flying down and calming our friend the turtle. Thanks to you he is now happy and smiling." The pigeon went on and told his friend the butterfly, "I was once saved at the last moment, too, when a **Snake** that was hiding in the leaves here almost got me, but I escaped."

"I have an idea," said the **Pigeon**. "Let's have a party for the rabbit that was saved from the jaws of the evil lion. We'll have healthy snacks and fruits, and we'll also invite the **Rabbit** and **Turtle** to play with us."

And that's the way it was. They all went to play on the **Slide**, then sailed the **Boat**, and finally had a big festive **Table** with healthy fruits. And they all sat together for a feast, in honor of the elephant who wasn't afraid of the lion.

Butterfly

Wave hands and knees up and down 10 times

Lying Pigeon

Inhale, head up, hold for 5 breaths on each foot

Snake

Bend elbows, feet together, breathe 5 breaths

Table

Maintain high stomach, hold for 8 breaths

Boat

Sit, back straight, hold for 8 breaths

Slide

Inhale, strong stomach upward, hold for 5 breaths

Mountain

Body held straight and stretched, look towards palms, hold for 8 breaths

Tree

Sole of foot on thigh, hands up, hold for 5 breaths for each foot

Rabbit

Inhale, head down, hold for 5 breaths

Lying Pigeon

Inhale, head up, hold for 5 breaths on each foot

Shawana the Brave Dog

On a tall **Mountain**, in a great forest full of **Trees**, there was a small village with a petting zoo in it.

At the petting zoo there were **Rabbits**, **Pigeons**, **Fish**, and even a **Camel**; it was always nice for all of them to play there.

The petting zoo was guarded by a small but brave **Dog** called Shawana, who would bark especially loud. He was a good friend to all the nice animals at the petting zoo.

Life there was beautiful, but could sometimes be scary, because every once in a while, predators would try and get in and catch the nice animals.

Fish

Palms beneath buttocks, shoulders up, hold for 10 breaths

Camel

Lift chest up, hold for 5 breaths

Downward Facing Dog

Raise hips, stretch heels towards the mat, hold for 5 breaths

Eagle

Knee slightly bent, hold for 5 breaths on each foot

When that would happen, the brave little **Dog** Shawana would do his job and guard the petting zoo and his friends from the scary animals. He was so brave that no animal dared fight him, not even the big ones.

Above the petting zoo was a huge **Tree**, and its green leaves shaded the animals. One day, a great **Eagle** arrived, stood on a branch, and eagerly looked at the little **Rabbits**, longing to taste one of them. The rabbits got scared and silently squeaked, but Shawana the **Dog** – who had great ears – heard them. He looked up, noticed the **Eagle**, and started barking his loud barks at him, making the dangerous **Eagle** run away from the petting zoo, and never come back.

Rabbit

Inhale, head down, hold for 5 breaths

Slide

Inhale, strong stomach upward, hold for 5 breaths

Lizard

Relaxation pose, hold for 10 breaths, and switch sides

All the animals were happy because the **Rabbits** were safe, and they went to celebrate on the **Slide**. Then they all went to sleep like **Lizards**, until the morning.

The following day, a dangerous **Cobra** entered the petting zoo silently. He quietly whispered and rattled towards the animals, and even sent out his long tongue to try to swallow the **Pigeons**.

Luckily for the friends, Shawana the **Dog** heard the frightened flaps of the pigeons' wings this time as well, looked down at the **Snake**, and barked at him. Then Shawana the **Dog** barked again with his loud and scary voice, until the **Snake** got scared, and ran away back into the forest.

All the animals were happy that the pigeons were saved, and they celebrated at the **Boat**, and then they all went to sleep in a **Frog** position, until the morning.

Downward Facing Dog

Snake

Bend elbows, feet together, breathe 5 breaths

Lying Flat

Lie on back, eyes closed, body relaxed, hold for 20 breaths

Downward Facing Dog

Raise hips, heels stretching towards the mat, hold for 5 breaths

Boat

Sit, back straight, hold for 8 breaths

The scariest thing happened one evening, when a big **Lion** stood outside the petting zoo fence and rocked the chain with his great paw, roared loudly, looked at the **Camel**, and wanted to eat it. The camel made a frightened wheeze and went silent with fear. Shawana the **Dog** arrived after hearing the wheezing and roaring. He was not scared or afraid, only stood in front of the **Lion** and barked back at him, until the lion understood that Shawana the **Dog** would not give up so easily and he decided to go back to the forest.

After he left, the animals were very happy. Shawana the **Dog** and all his friends from the petting zoo, the **Pigeons**, the **Camel**, the **Rabbits**, and even the **Fish** celebrated together. Once they got tired, they lay on their **Backs**, happy, and closed their eyes with very big smiles spread across their faces.

Upward Facing Dog

Frog

Hands under thighs, grasping ankles, hold for 10 breaths

Lion

Sit on heels, back straight, extend tongue while inhaling and roar

Camel

Lift chest up, hold for 5 breaths

Lying Flat

Lie on back, eyes closed, body relaxed, hold for 20 breaths

Fish

Palms beneath buttocks, shoulders up, hold for 10 breaths

Lying Pigeon

Inhale, head up, hold for 5 breaths on each foot

Upward Facing Dog

Hands straight, thighs in the air, hold for 5 breaths

The Camel and the Giant Bamboo Tree

Mauna Training and Practice

"I miss my friend the **Elephant**," the huge **Camel** thought to himself as he stood sad and lonely in the scorching desert, looking for some shade and friends to play with. From afar he saw the giant bamboo **Tree** and decided to go there. He walked and walked (Stride silently and slowly for about thirty seconds, noticing as you place each and every step) and suddenly he met his friend the Rabbit.

"Camel, buddy, where are you going?" the rabbit asked the **Camel**.

"I'm hot. I am going to the giant Tree in the distance, to rest in its shade."

Elephant trunk up

Inhale, hands up

Camel

Lift chest up, hold for 5 breaths

"I am also hot," said the **Snake**, "can I join you?" he asked the **Camel** and **Rabbit**.

"Certainly. Let's all walk together," the two answered and the three of them started **walking quietly** again. And so the three friends slowly walked in the scorching heat of the desert, until they suddenly met an old friend – the **Lizard**.

"Hello, my friends," said the lizar. "Where are you walking to so slowly?" she asked and lay on her tummy on the hot sand, while turning her head away from them.

"We are walking to the giant bamboo **Tree**, to enjoy its shade," answered the **Camel**, **Rabbit**, and **Snake.**

"Can I walk with you, too?" the lizard asked and stretched out her tail in anticipation. "Sure you can," the three answered and the four of them kept walking **slowly**, until they reached the giant **Tree**.

When they arrived, they saw their good friend the black **Eagle** at the treetop. He seemed very sad, and he told them, "The giant bamboo tree is very sick since a big and thorny

Camel

cactus grew right on its trunk, drinking away all the water it needs. It is in pain and might die."

When the friends heard the news, they all became very sad; only the **Camel** did not seem worried.

"Friends, do not worry, I can save the tree; my lips and teeth are very strong and do not get pricked by any cactus. I can have it for breakfast," the **Camel** said. He sat on all fours, the way camels do when they eat cacti, and began eating the prickly cactus with appetite, while making sounds of joy: "ah-ah-ah-ah." By evening, there was nothing left of the cactus, and the giant bamboo **Tree** began growing again and smiling with joy.

The five friends – the **Camel**, the **Rabbit**, the **Snake**, the **Lizard**, and the **Eagle** – were so happy to see that the giant **Tree** was blooming again, that they decided to have a party. They celebrated by playing on the sand **Slide** on the nearby dune, and when night fell, they all lay down to sleep like their friend the **Lizard** and had a good night's sleep.

Lizard

Mountain

Body held straight and stretched, look towards palms, hold for 8 breaths

Tree

Sole of foot on thigh, hands up, hold for 5 breaths for each foot

Owl

Sit straight on heels, eyes moving left and right 10 times

Bee

Back leg stretched in the air, hold for 5 breaths for each foot

The Brave Bees

On top of a low **Mountain** grew a big and tall **Tree**, and in a big nest hidden on one of its branches, the **Owl** raised her owlets in peace and quiet.

On the same **Tree** was a hive, home to the good-hearted **Bees**.

The **Owl** was grumpy and did not like the **Bees**, since their loud buzzing bothered her and her owlets.

Beneath the **Tree** stood a small **Table**, under which Shawana the **Dog** liked to nap. He would sleep there all day in the shade, and enjoy his wonderful life. When he woke up, he faced down and stretched; sometimes

Table
Maintain high stomach, hold for 8 breaths

Downward Facing Dog
Raise hips, heels stretching towards the mat, hold for 5 breaths

Upward Facing Dog
Hands straight, thighs in the air, hold for 5 breaths

Cat, Back Arched
Exhale and hold without breathing, repeat 5 times

he would face up towards the **Owl** and the **Bees**.

One morning, a big and mischievous **Cat** came by and saw Shawana the dog sleeping peacefully in his usual place, under the **Table**. The **Cat** decided to play a trick on the dog: he snuck behind Shawana, hit him on the head, and hid behind the tree trunk.

Shawana the **Dog** woke up with fright, faced down and couldn't see anyone, faced up and couldn't see anyone either. 'I may have dreamt it,' he thought to himself and got back to his nap.

Owl

Sit straight on heels, eyes moving left and right 10 times

Bee

Back leg stretched in the air, hold for 5 breaths for each foot

Tree

Sole of foot on thigh, hands up, hold for 5 breaths for each foot

The mischievous **Cat** saw that Shawana the dog was napping again, and decided to repeat his trick. He slowly came closer and hit the **Dog** on the head again. This time, Shawana woke up immediately, just in time to see the sly cat's tail wiggling behind the tree trunk.

The dog was very mad and started chasing the naughty cat around the **Tree** trunk, until the cat had no choice but to climb up the tree quickly, not noticing that he scared the **Owl** and her owlets. The owl was so scared, she immediately flew off the nest, leaving the owlets all alone.

Slowly, the cat was making himself comfortable on the tree. He looked around and saw the nest, hidden among the leaves, and the lonely owlets in it. The cat had a bad thought: 'Someone sent me nice owlets for breakfast,' he thought to himself and he started approaching them, so he could eat them.

The **Owl** was horrified by the fate of her owlets and started waving her wings, moving her eyes from side to side quickly. But that did not deter the naughty **Cat**, who kept moving

Cat, Back Arched

towards the owlets until he faced them, drew out his nails, and was about to stick them into the poor owlets.

Suddenly, help came from an unexpected source. The **Bees**, who saw what was about to happen, decided to defend the owlets. They flew over to the naughty cat by the dozens, buzzing loudly next to his ears. They buzzed by his nostrils, they buzzed by his lips, they buzzed by his feet. The cat did not quit and tried to fight back, until one smart little **Bee** stung him on his behind.

The **Cat** was startled and wept loudly, got down from the tall tree, started running, and disappeared.

The owl, who understood the bees were good and helpful, thanked them and was no longer angry at them. She let the **Bees** buzz whenever they wanted and became their best friend.

Ever since then, the **Owl**, **Bees**, and Shawana the **Dog** all live quietly and peacefully on and under the big **Tree**, and the naughty **Cat** does not dare come back.

Cat, Back Bowed

Windmill

On exhaling, cross arm to opposite leg, inhale and come up, exhale and cross other hand to other leg. Repeat 5 times.

Eagle

Knee slightly bent, hold for 5 breaths on each foot

Lying Pigeon

Inhale, head up, hold for 5 breaths on each foot

Tree

Sole of foot on thigh, hands up, hold for 5 breaths for each foot

The Eagle and the Pigeon

There was once a tall **Windmill** on a small farm, its giant blades always turning thanks to the strong winds.

At the end of the summer, a large **Eagle** arrived there and built his nest on the pointy top of the tall **Windmill**, without knowing that at the small window below him lived a beautiful **Pigeon** hatching two small eggs.

Under the **Windmill** grew a big **Tree**, and between its leaves, in hidden burrows in the trunk, a family of **Bees** and **Butterflies** lived peacefully, each having its own burrow.

Bee

Back leg stretched in the air, hold for 5 breaths for each foot

Butterfly

Wave hands and knees up and down 10 times

Rabbit

Inhale, head down, hold for 5 breaths

Turtle

Hold position while inhaling for 5 breaths

Under the **Tree**, in a narrow burrow, lived a mother rabbit, father **Rabbit**, and their twelve mischievous little rabbits. On the other side of the **Tree** lived a family of **Turtles**: a father turtle, mother turtle, and three little sleepy turtles, who lived a good life. The turtle family was the rabbit family's good friends and neighbors, and they all lived there in peace and quiet.

It was nice and cozy for everyone at the farm throughout the summer, until winter came along and brought with it strong and very cold winds. The **Windmill**'s blades turned even faster, and the eagle no longer felt safe. He suffered from the strong winds.

Eagle

Knee slightly bent, hold for 5 breaths on each foot

Windmill

On exhaling, cross arm to opposite leg, inhale and come up, exhale and cross other hand to other leg. Repeat 5 times.

Tree

Sole of foot on thigh, hands up, hold for 5 breaths for each foot

Bee

Back leg stretched in the air, hold for 5 breaths for each foot

Butterfly

Wave hands and knees up and down 10 times

One day, a storm blew. The **Eagle** got very cold and he could no longer stay at the top of the **Windmill**, so he flew from his nest to the **Tree**'s leaves and tried to shelter himself from the strong wind. But he couldn't. The wind was so strong that the **Eagle** asked the **Bees** to let him hide with them in their hive, inside the tree trunk.

"No, no! It is narrow; we are sorry, but you cannot come in," the bees said.

Disappointed, the eagle went to the **Butterflies** and asked to come into their burrow inside the **Tree** trunk. But they also said, "We are sorry, dear eagle, our house is also narrow, and we cannot fit you in."

Sadly, the eagle went down to the **Rabbits** and asked to hide in their burrow with them. But mother rabbit said, "We are a large family and the space is too narrow even for us, so, dear eagle, you cannot come in."

The **Eagle** looked at the **Turtle** family and saw that they each carried their home on their backs, and it was clear that he could not squeeze himself in there. The eagle was desperate.

Suddenly, he had an idea: 'I will hide at the small window at the top of the **Windmill**.' He decided to fly there, despite the strong wind, and try to get in.

The **Eagle** spread his wings and flew to the window and saw that the glass was closed; through the glass he saw the beautiful **Pigeon** sleeping in her warm nest, along with her two newly hatched chicks.

While practicing yoga, proper breathing is of the utmost importance and must be maintained.

The **Eagle** was desperate, but despite that, he knocked politely on the glass with his beak. The beautiful **Pigeon** woke up and saw that the **Eagle** was in distress, since the strong wind was about to blow him onto the **Windmill's** rotating blades, and that would be quite bad.

When the good-hearted **Pigeon** saw that, she did not think twice and opened the window for the **Eagle**, allowing him to come in where it was warm. The eagle thanked the beautiful and kind-hearted **Pigeon**. He stood at the far corner where he spread his wings and slowly dried off, enjoying the warmth of the place. Later, tired and weary, he lay down and slept until the morning.

The following morning, the sun shone again. The **Eagle** woke up first. He felt grateful and decided he had to repay the pigeon's kind-heartedness. Slowly, he opened the window and flew to the nearest field, where he gathered seeds and grains with his great beak, filled it up, went back to the window, and placed them by the beautiful **Pigeon**, who was still asleep in her nest with her chicks.

Eventually, the **Eagle** returned to his nest and since then, he never forgot what the noble **Pigeon** had done for him; each morning he would fly and gather a beakful of seeds and grains and place them beside her, before she would wake up.

That way, the eagle repaid the good-hearted pigeon for her great help.

Lying Pigeon

Inhale, head up, hold for 5 breaths on each foot

Rabbit

Inhale, head down, hold for 5 breaths

Turtle

Hold position while inhaling for 5 breaths

During exercises, inhale and exhale only through the nose.

Eagle

Knee slightly bent, hold for 5 breaths on each foot

Windmill

On exhaling, cross arm to opposite leg, inhale and come up, exhale and cross other hand to other leg. Repeat 5 times.

Mountain

Body held straight and stretched, look towards palms, hold for 8 breaths

Fish

Palms beneath buttocks, shoulders up, hold for 10 breaths

Turtle

Hold position while inhaling for 5 breaths

Swan

Stomach close to mat, hands straight, hold for 5 breaths

The Noble Swan

At a magical lake, at the foot of a tall **Mountain**, a **Fish**, a water **Turtle**, and a white **Swan** lived peacefully.

Each morning, a small baby **Elephant** would come to the lake, along with his family of elephants, to drink from the lake and bathe in it.

When the baby **Elephant** would arrive, the **Fish**, **Turtle**, and **Swan** would patiently wait beside the lake, until the family of elephants would finish what they were doing and get out of the water. When they left, only

the baby **Elephant** would stay in the water and happily and loudly play with his friends.

On the other side of the lake were small **Boats**, but they never made it to where the four good friends played.

The four friends would go up the water **Slide** and quickly slide down in the strong stream. They would then go on a small **Boat** and row around, playing and loudly having fun; before saying goodbye, they would get a joyful shower from the baby **Elephant**'s trunk.

One morning, the three good friends, the **Fish**, **Turtle**, and **Swan**, waited

Elephant trunk up/down
Inhale, hands up/exhale, hands down.

Boat
Sit, back straight, hold for 8 breaths

Slide
Inhale, strong stomach upward, hold for 5 breaths

Elephant trunk up/down

Inhale, hands up/exhale, hands down

Fish

Palms beneath buttocks, shoulders up, hold for 10 breaths

Turtle

Hold position while inhaling for 5 breaths

Swan

Stomach close to mat, hands straight, hold for 5 breaths

for the baby **Elephant** in the water near the beach. That morning, the baby elephant and his family were late.

After a long wait, the **Fish** told his friends the **Turtle** and **Swan**: "Let's swim along the beach, we might meet the baby elephant on his way here." The friends agreed and started swimming after the Fish along the beach, between bushes and **Trees**.

The friends swam away from where they always roamed and did not realize someone dangerous was following them, waiting for the opportunity to jump up and eat them. The dangerous creature was their enemy the **Alligator**, who was waiting for an opportunity to eat the three friends. It was only thanks to the baby elephant, who was always around, that he never dared to come close to them. Now, seeing that the baby elephant was not with them, the **Alligator** decided it was time to attack.

The **Alligator** quietly swam after the three friends. When he saw they were swimming by the tall water bushes, he decided to hide behind the **Tree** trunk and wait.

The **Fish** swam first and passed the **Tree** trunk, the **Turtle** followed him, but nothing happened, but when the **Swan** passed the **Tree** trunk, the **Alligator** jumped at the **Swan** and tried to grab him with his teeth.

But the swan was smarter and quicker than the **Alligator**. He began swimming quickly to where he came from, to get

Swan

the alligator away from his two friends, the **Fish** and **Turtle**, who did not see the danger coming.

The **Swan** swam with all his strength to where they always waited for the baby elephant, but since the **Alligator** had a long tail, he caught up to him and the **Swan** felt his stamina running out.

The **Alligator** was moving fast, and the **Swan** realized he was about to get caught and accepted his fate. And then, a moment before it happened, the baby **Elephant** arrived there with his family, ran towards the swan, and stepped on the **Alligator**'s tail, making him turn around and swim quickly away.

When the **Fish** and **Turtle** arrived, the **Swan** was breathing hard in fatigue. They had noticed the **Swan** was not behind them and backtracked to look for him. They arrived just as the baby **Elephant** scared the evil **Alligator** away.

The good friends, the baby **Elephant**, **Fish**, and **Turtle**, immediately understood that their friend the good **Swan** swam the other way in order to save the fish and turtle from danger, and they thanked the brave swan for his noble act.

After also thanking the baby elephant for saving the swan, the friends returned to playing together, as they always did. They slid down the water **Slide**, climbed on the **Boat** and sailed it, and later the baby elephant carried them around the water.

Fish

Tree

Sole of foot on thigh, hands up, hold for 5 breaths for each foot

Alligator

Strong stretching of the body, arms to ears, hold for 10 breaths

Slide

Inhale, strong stomach upward, hold for 5 breaths

Boat

Sit, back straight, hold for 8 breaths

Warrior

Forward knee bent, hold for 10 breaths for each side

Tree

Sole of foot on thigh, hands up, hold for 5 breaths for each foot

Monkey

Legs stretched forward and back, hold for 10 breaths for each foot

The Warrior Who Guarded the Forest

In a great big jungle lived a **Warrior**, who was a good friend to all the animals, the trees, and the plants. He built his home on top of the tallest **Tree** in the forest and would overlook everything around.

At the warrior's home, at the top of the tall tree, lived a **Monkey**. His name was Anoman, and he was the **Warrior**'s best friend. Each morning, when he saw the warrior, the **Monkey** would greet him, "Hello," as he stood

on his legs, banging himself on the chest and saying, "Woo Haa Ei Ooo, Woo Haa Ei Oo." He always did this a few times.

Anoman the monkey was trained and made sure to pick up and gather food for the warrior: various nuts, fruits, and roots. He would do it while swinging from one **Tree** to the next, in a funny way and quite quickly.

After Amoman the **Monkey** would gather food for the **Warrior**, he would climb up and place the food in a large bowl set on the wooden **Table**, which the warrior built.

Table

Maintain high stomach, hold for 8 breaths

Elephant trunk up

Inhale, hands up

Elephant trunk down

Exhale, lean down

Warrior
Forward knee bent, hold for 10 breaths for each side

Rider
Wide stance, knees bent, back straight, bend knees lower and then straighten, repeat 10 times

Bow and Arrow
Lower knee bent, face upper hand, hold for 10 breaths on each side

Elephant trunk up/down
Inhale, hands up. Exhale, lean down

Lion
Sit on heels, back straight, extend tongue while inhaling and roar

Boat

The **Warrior** was also good friends with a big **Elephant** called Ganesh, who was the leader of the elephants in the forest. He would **Ride** him every day, roam the forest, and make sure that everything was going well. When the warrior wanted Ganesh the elephant to arrive, he would whistle loudly "*Fweeeet*," and the elephant would hear him and come.

When the **Warrior** would leave his home, he always took his **Bow** and arrows with him, in case he might need them in the forest, which could be dangerous.

Each morning, the **Warrior** would go out to tour the giant forest on the back of Ganesh the **Elephant**. Anoman the **Monkey** would always join them and sit on the great **Elephant** Ganesh's back, along with the warrior. Since Ganesh would start galloping, the warrior would hold tightly to his ears, so he wouldn't fall back, and so they galloped "*Dumm dugudum*."

One day, after an hour of riding through the forest, they reached a clearing and saw something unusual happening. A great **Lion** and a huge **Cobra** were standing in front of each other in a threatening pose. The **Lion** roared at the **Cobra**, and the snake lifted himself up, as if ready to attack the lion. Without hesitating, the brave **Warrior** jumped off the elephant's back with his **Bow**, stood between the **Lion** and the **Cobra**, and stopped them from attacking each other.

The **Warrior** listened to the claims of the **Lion** and **Cobra** against each other, funny and silly claims about who would move first and let the other one pass through. The wise **Warrior** asked each of them to move a bit to the right, clearing the way so they could each move on, and a brutal and unnecessary fight was prevented.

From there, the gang – the **Elephant**, **Monkey**, and **Warrior** – continued to bathe in the lake and drink from its water. The **Elephant** filled his trunk with water and surprised them by spraying a strong jet of water at them from behind. It was a funny thing, which made Anoman the monkey jump with joy and once again yell, "Woo Haa Ei Ooo, Woo Haa Ei Oo."

After they drank and bathed, the **Warrior** put his canoe **Boat**, which he had made out of an old tree trunk, into the lake and rowed, using a long paddle, to a small island where the **Lotus** flower grew. He picked one white and extraordinarily beautiful flower so he could bring it to his treetop house.

The daily trip ended, the **Warrior** and the **Monkey** slowly rode on the elephant and returned home together. The warrior climbed quickly to the top of the **Tree**, placed the lotus flower in a pot with water, and then sat in front of it in a **Lotus** pose. He closed his eyes and sank into a pleasant meditation, picturing the white beautiful flower and only listening to his breaths, twenty of them.

Snake
Bend elbows, feet together, breathe 5 breaths

Monkey
Legs stretched forward and back, hold for 10 breaths for each foot

Boat
Sit, back straight, hold for 8 breaths

Table

Tree
Sole of foot on thigh, hands up, hold for 5 breaths for each foot

Lotus
Soles of feet atop each other, back straight, eyes closed, breathe 20 breaths

Stretch Up

On inhale, stretch arms up while looking at palms

Stretch Down

On exhale, bow down

Half-Stretch

On inhale, raise body high, palms to knees

Runner

Front leg bent, back leg stretched, back stretched

The Animal Farm

In a little farm in nature, many animals lived together in peace. Each morning, as the sun shone, the farmer would leave his house and perform the **Sun Salutation**; this greeting was composed of several yoga poses, with a preset order:

Tad – starting pose;
Stretch up;
Stretch down;
Half-stretch;
Runner;
Beam;
Chest touching the ground;
Upward facing dog;
Downward facing dog;

**Runner;
Half-stretch down;
Stretch down;
Stretch up;
Tad – starting pose.**

After he finished performing the **Sun Salutation**, once to the left and once to the right, the farmer would go and feed the animals on the farm

He always started with the **Horses**, which were already awake, because they slept through the night standing up. Later, he went on to feed the **Pigeons**, the **Rabbits**, the **Turtles**, and finally the **Dogs**, whose job was to herd the small farm's **Cows**.

Beam

Body straight and stretched

Chest Touching the Ground

On exhale, knees, chest, and chin down to mat

Upward Facing Dog

Hands straight, thighs in the air, hold for 5 breaths

Downward Facing Dog

Raise hips, heels stretching towards the mat, hold for 5 breaths

Horse (Rider)
Wide stance, knees bent, back straight, bend knees lower and then straighten, repeat 10 times

Lying Pigeon
Inhale, head up, hold for 5 breaths on each foot

Rabbit
Inhale, head down, hold for 5 breaths

When he would finish, the farmer would sit down in a **Lotus** pose and eat his breakfast with his family. Later, he would mount his **Horse** and ride, "Digidam digidam," to the meadow with the herd of **Cows** and the two dogs, one **Dog** looking up and the other **Dog** looking down.

When they arrived at the meadow, the farmer would descend from his **Horse** and would **Lie Down** to rest, on his back, under a large **Tree**. He would close his eyes and fall right asleep; he would rest like that for a whole hour.

One day, shortly after he lay down to rest, the farmer was awoken by a few short barks. When he opened his eyes, he saw the two dogs, who were looking after the **Cows** in the meadow, standing next to him. The upward facing **Dog** was barking loudly to wake his master from sleep, and the other one – the downward facing **Dog** – was clutching onto the farmer's pants, and they both tried to get his attention.

The farmer immediately understood that something was wrong. He looked around and saw that his **Horse** was at the same place he had left him; he looked at the **Cows** and saw they were all there, but one of them was lying on its side. The farmer came closer to see why the cow was lying on its side, and saw that she was giving birth to a small calf. His legs were already out, but she seemed to be in pain and needed help.

The farmer got to his knees, and started pulling the small calf out of the suffering **Cow**'s belly, until he was out and laid next to his mother, in the **Fetal** position, resting from the exhausting birth.

Turtle
Hold position while inhaling for 5 breaths

Lotus
Soles of feet atop each other, back straight, eyes closed, breathe 20 breaths

Cow
Sitting on one heel, other leg over the knee, hold for 10 breaths and switch sides

Stretch Up
On inhale, stretch arms up while looking at palms

The farmer looked at the **Cow** and saw that it was still lying exhausted. He went to his **Horse**, took out a bottle of water from the saddle, and went back to give water to the **Cow**, which slowly started to recover. She lifted her head a bit and looked at the little calf she just gave birth to, but she still lay there, very weak.

The farmer, who saw that the mother could not lick her newborn clean as she should, got up, picked a few leaves from the nearby **Tree**, and cleaned the calf's body with them.

All that time, the two **Dogs** sat and quietly watched. When they saw the farmer cleaning the little calf's body with the green leaves, they both came to help him and licked the calf with their tongues, as if it was their own puppy. It was a moving sight that the farmer would forever remember.

Slowly, the **Cow** regained her strength and rose to her feet, still wobbling with imbalance. The little calf, who saw his mom rising to her feet, followed her lead and also rose up. He approached his mother, wobbling, mooing softly, and getting soft moos back from the weak mother.

The farmer was happy. He sat back down, this time in a **Lotus** pose, and looked at how the calf was searching for his mother's udder, which was full of milk, and suckling on the fresh and healthy milk.

The farmer joyfully looked at the lovely sight and was happy that he had been blessed to save the **Cow** and calf with the help of the smart dogs – the downward facing **Dog** and the upward facing **Dog**.

Upward Facing Dog
Hands straight, thighs in the air, hold for 5 breaths

Downward Facing Dog
Raise hips, heels stretching towards the mat, hold for 5 breaths

Tree
Sole of foot on thigh, hands up, hold for 5 breaths for each foot

Stretch Down
On exhale, bow down

Fetal
Relaxation pose, hold for 12 breaths with body relaxed

Sitting Hero
Sit straight, eyes closed, hold for 12 breaths

Lying Flat
Lie on back, eyes closed, body relaxed, hold for 20 breaths

Tree
Sole of foot on thigh, hands up, hold for 5 breaths for each foot

Downward Facing Dog
Raise hips, heels stretching towards the mat, hold for 5 breaths

Cat, Back Bowed
Inhale and hold breath, repeat 5 times

Half-Moon

At a faraway land, in a beautiful valley full of green plants and **Trees**, lay a small picturesque town. The people in that town loved animals very much, which is why many **Dogs** and **Cats** roamed the streets.

In this town, the **Cows** were considered holy, which is why they could walk around freely, and no one ever hurt them.

The town's buildings looked like temples and had many **Elephants** sculpted on their walls; the sculpted elephants would at times seem to be drinking from the river, raising their trunks up and spraying their surroundings, symbolizing wisdom.

Cow
Sitting on one heel, other leg over the knee, hold for 10 breaths and switch sides

Elephant trunk up
Inhale, hands up

Elephant trunk down
Exhale, lean down

The temples' walls had many images of colorful gods sculpted on them, and even **Cobras**, which symbolized spiritual wisdom in the town.

At the center of town was a great and wide river named the Ganges. It was considered holy by the residents of the town and had many colorful **Boats** on it, moving through the river lightly and nobly, their white sails appearing like the shiny wings of white **Pigeons**.

In the middle of town, above the river, towered a great and wide **Bridge**, and the people washing in the river

Snake
Bend elbows, feet together, breathe 5 breaths

Boat
Sit, back straight, hold for 8 breaths

Lying Pigeon
Inhale, head up, hold for 5 breaths on each foot

Lying Flat
Lie on back, eyes closed, body relaxed, hold for 20 breaths

Bridge
Lie on back, hands behind shoulders, bring soles of feet towards buttocks, and on exhale raise stomach and head upward, hold for 5 breaths

Bridge
Lie on back, hands behind shoulders, bring soles of feet towards buttocks, and on exhale raise stomach and head upward, hold for 5 breaths

Tree
Sole of foot on thigh, hands up, hold for 5 breaths for each foot

Mountain
Body held straight and stretched, look towards palms, hold for 8 breaths

Flower Wreath
From standing, sit down, buttocks off the mat, hold for 5 breaths

would go under the bridge to **Rest** in its shade, away from the heavy summer heat.

Each day, a young girl would arrive under the **Bridge**. She came there to sell a tasty and refreshing lemon drink to the people who rested under the bridge, which her grandmother made from the lemon **Tree** in her garden. That is how the girl helped her grandmother make a living.

The girl's name was Emily and she could not remember her parents, since she had lost them in an accident when she was a baby, and had been living with her grandmother ever since. When Emily was asked, "Where are your parents?" she would always answer, "When I was little, they went up to the top of the high **Volcano** and up to the sky; now they are looking down and watching over me."

When winter would come and it got too cold for the juice of the lemon **Tree**, Emily would bring bundles of flowers under the **Bridge**, from which she and her grandmother would make **Wreaths** and sell them to the people who sat under the bridge to shelter themselves from the cold.

The people who bought the wreaths laid them on a small **Tree** trunk, that looked like a **Half-Moon**, and in its center

Bridge

placed a **Candle**. The candle would light up the **Wreaths** and the **Half-Moon** tree trunk in a beautiful and colorful light.

Towards the evening, when the moon would rise and light the wide river with its silver light, the people would place the little tree trunks on the water, light the **Candles** at their center, and ask for a wish or to bless someone; they believed that their wish would come true. That is how hundreds of candles floated on the holy river each evening and with them hundreds of wishes, giving the place a festive atmosphere, which made everyone happy.

It was a joyous sight for Emily. Even though she lived with her grandmother, without her parents, she felt happy and lucky since she shared the hope and joy of the people who would come to sail the **Wreaths** with the lit **Candles** on the river each evening.

Once the people finished the ceremony, they went back to their homes to rest for the night – some walked, and some took a **Boat** home.

That was also when Emily would go back to her grandmother's house, and after a shower, she would eat and tell her grandmother everything she had done throughout the day. Then, she would **Lay Down to Sleep**, smiling.

Half-Moon

Warrior stance, lower hand to mat, raise leg, hold for 5 breaths

Candle

Lie on back, roll legs towards head, support back, hold for 5 breaths

Boat

Sit, back straight, hold for 8 breaths

Lying Flat

Lie on back, eyes closed, body relaxed, hold for 20 breaths

Half-Moon

The Golden-Winged Crane

Warrior

Forward knee bent, hold for 10 breaths for each side

Tree

Sole of foot on thigh, hands up, hold for 5 breaths for each foot

Bow and Arrow

Lower knee bent, face upper hand, hold for 10 breaths on each side

Many years ago, there was a big city surrounded by walls. The city was very famous since it had a brave **Warrior** living in it. His name was Vira Badra, meaning the Hero Badra.

The warrior was at the disposal of the city's king, was very loyal to him, went on the toughest missions for him, and did all he ever asked him to.

One morning, the king called Badra the **Hero** to him and said, "I heard that in the fields outside the city, between the tall **Trees**, there is a great white bird with golden wings. I do not know the bird's name, but I am asking you to go out to the fields, hunt it, and bring it to me, alive."

Badra bowed to the king, took his **Bow** and arrows and left for the mission at once. He saddled his coal-black **Horse**, mounted it, and rode towards the city **Gate**.

When the guards at the gate saw Badra the **Hero** riding their way on his black **Horse**, they immediately lowered their heads in respect, bowed down, and opened the **Gate** for him.

Badra rode on to the fields, and the further he got from the city, the more he feared he would not be able to capture the golden-winged bird the king had spoken about.

He rode his **Horse** far, and by noon arrived at the great forest filled with giant **Trees**. 'Maybe the golden-winged bird is hiding between the forest trees,' thought Badra the **Hero** and decided to ride into the forest, to look for it there.

Horse (Rider)
Wide stance, knees bent, back straight, bend knees lower and then straighten, repeat 10 times

Closed Gate
Hands stretched to sides, hold for 5 breaths for each side

Open Gate
Stretch arm parallel to ear, hold for 5 breaths on each side

He rode his **Horse** on the narrow path. He looked up, looked to the sides, but there was no trace of the mysterious bird. And so, his horse walked the path until it came to a round clearing, where Badra dismounted his horse. He noticed a single flower, remarkable in its beauty, all white, its petals looking like a royal crown.

That was the rare **Lotus** flower, a flower which did not grow there but at far away places, near water springs.

Badra the hero sat in front of the beautiful **Lotus** flower, closed his eyes, put his hands together, pressed them to his chest, and focused on thinking of the mysterious bird. He asked himself, 'Is it hiding in this forest?' and the answer from his heart was, 'No, it is not here.'

The **Warrior** opened his eyes, got up and looked at the flower one last time. Then he mounted his **Horse** and went back on the path he came from. He left the forest and rode to the far fields, where he saw an old man sitting at the edge of the field, with his hat covering his eyes.

Badra dismounted his horse, went to the man, bowed a **Deep Bow**, and respectfully asked, "Dear sir, do you know where I can find the golden-winged bird?"

The man took off his hat, looked at Badra the hero and said, "You must mean the golden-winged **Crane**. It is a majestic bird and does not show itself to ordinary people, but only to brave warriors. Keep riding with your **Horse** behind that far **Mountain**, there between the trees, you will find it. If you prove to be a **Hero**, it will reveal itself to you."

Badra pressed his hands together, close to his chest, and thanked the old man with a **Deep Bow**. "What is your name, dear sir?" Badra asked the old man. "My name is **Marichi**," the old man answered and went on, "Sit with me for a while and then go on your way." Badra did as he asked, sat by the wise man, and they both closed their eyes and breathed slowly.

When they were done, the two parted ways. Badra mounted his **Horse** and rode like the wind towards the high **Mountain**, and shortly before the sun set, he reached its beautiful peak.

Badra the warrior saw the line of **Trees** the wise **Marichi** talked about and dismounted his horse. He looked at the trees and waited peacefully, as if he knew the mysterious bird would soon reveal itself to him.

After a long wait, a large bird emerged from the trees. It flew over and landed at Badra the brave **Hero**'s feet. It was a big snow-white **Crane**. The bird looked at him, and when it was sure he would not hurt it, started to dance the crane dance before him.

"It is not the bird I am looking for," the disappointed Badra thought. "It has no golden wings."

But, at that moment, the sun began to set and painted everything golden red, like the color of the sunset. Badra the hero looked at the white crane, dancing in front of him, and its wings were painted bright gold– amazingly beautiful.

Badra the **Hero** was amazed by the **Crane**'s beauty. Immediately he lowered his eyes and bowed to the beautiful bird. When he looked up, instead of the golden crane stood the most beautiful girl he had ever seen.

"You, who didn't try to hunt me with your **Bow** and arrows, proved that you are a true **Hero** and broke the spell."

Badra looked at the beautiful princess and said, "I fell in love with you at first sight and I ask you to marry me. Together we will build our home here, on top of the **Mountain**, and I will never again serve the king, who sent me to hunt you."

The beautiful princess agreed to Badra the **Hero**'s offer, married him, and together they built their home on top of the high **Mountain**, where they lived happily ever after, surrounded by **Trees** and beautiful **Lotus** flowers.

Crane
Place palms under shoulders, raise one knee to the elbow, then the other, balance using abdominal muscles, hold for 3 breaths

Mountain
Body held straight and stretched, look towards palms, hold for 8 breaths

Tree
Sole of foot on thigh, hands up, hold for 5 breaths for each foot

Marichi
Back straight, look towards shoulder, rotate lower back, hold for 8 breaths and switch sides

Terms dictionary

The names of the drills are in Sanskrit (ancient Indian).

(Standing) Elephant – Arwahasta (hands up)

(Bent) Elephant – Otnasana (strong stretch)

Rabbit – Sasangasana

Lion – Simhasana

(Tall) Mountain – Tadasana

Tree – Vrksasana

Tortoise – Kurmasana

Butterfly – Baddha konasana

Cobra – Bhujangasana

Pigeon – Rajakapotasana (King Pigeon)

Slide – Purvottanasana (East)

Boat – Navasana

Table – Setuasana

Mouse – Mudra Yoga (Closing pose)

Lizard – Godaasana

Downward facing dog – Adho mukha svanasana

Upward facing dog – Urdhva mukha svanasana

Fish – Matsyasana

Camel – Ustrasana

Eagle – Garudasana

Frog – Mandhukasana

Cat/Cow – Marjaryasana (back down – Cat), Gomukhasana (back up – Cow)

Swan – Bhujangasana (tall Cobra pose)

Bee – Virabhadrasana 3 (named after the mythological warrior Badra)

Windmill – Parivrtta Trikonasana (triangle)

Owl – Tratkamasana

Walk – Mauna (meditative walk)

Monkey – Hanumanasana

Warrior – Virabhadrasana II

Crocodile – Makarasana

Rider – Ashwanyasana

Lotus – Padmasana

Mountain – Tadasana

Bow and Arrow – Vashistahasana

Cow – Gomukhasana

Half a stretch down – Ardha Uttanasana

Chest to the mat – Chaturanga (four contact points)

Runner – Parsvakonasana

Bridge – Urdhva dhanurasana (Upward facing bow)

Candle – Salabhasana Sarvangasana (Full body activity)

Garland – Malasana

Gate – Parighasana

Half a Moon – Ardha Chandrasana

Bow – Parsvottanasana

Marichi – Marichyasana III (Wiseman Marichi)

Crane – Bakasana